Who's Your Idol?™

CHRIS DAUGHTRY

Sandra Giddens

Published in 2008 by The Rosen Publishing Group, Inc.
29 East 21st Street, New York, NY 10010

Library of Congress Cataloging-in-Publication Data

Giddens, Sandra.
Chris Daughtry / Sandra Giddens. — 1st ed.
   p.cm. — (Who's your Idol?)
Includes bibliographical references (p. 45) and index.
ISBN-13: 978-1-4042-1371-5 (library binding)
1. Daughtry, Chris, 1979—Juvenile literature. 2. Rock musicians—
United States—Biography—Juvenile literature. I. Title.
ML3930.D325G53 2008
782.42166092—dc22

(B)

2007037749

Manufactured in the United States of America

Contents

Introduction

s there life after *American Idol*? Is it a fleeting moment of popularity, after which the glamour is gone, the applause stops, and the person goes back to his or her normal life? Or is there a chance that the show could propel the person to become a household name, with money and fame?

Welcome, Chris Daughtry. He was not the winner or even the runner-up on *American Idol* Season Five. In fact, he made it to the top ten and was eliminated by vote when it was down to just four finalists. He placed fourth behind Elliott Yamin, Katherine McPhee, and the eventual winner, Taylor Hicks. Many thought he was the most talented performer and should have gone all the way. But the amazing thing is that Chris Daughtry, or "the Rocker" as he was commonly called, has made it big, really big, and is still successful. He truly has become a star.

An excited Chris Daughtry attends a party in Los Angeles, California, in celebration of being one of *American Idol*'s top twelve contestants.

Be careful what you wish for,
'Cause you just might get it all.
You just might get it all,
And then some you don't want.
Be careful what you wish for,
'Cause you just might get it all.
You just might get it all.

Chris Daughtry wrote these lyrics to the song "Home." The producers of *American Idol* were so impressed with Daughtry's song that it replaced Daniel Powter's "Bad Day" as the final send-off for the sixth season. This is just one of his many successes after appearing on *American Idol*. In fact, his album *Daughtry* has been the fastest-selling debut rock album since SoundScan started tabulating sales in 1991. It sold almost two million copies in just sixteen weeks! The question to ask is, has he got it all?

Simon Cowell, in the book *I Don't Mean to Be Rude, But . . . ,* said that he himself has made millions from taking beginners with raw talent and turning those hopefuls into global pop stars through coaching and brutal honesty. Chris Daughtry has gone from being an unknown musician with plenty of raw talent to a well-known name to millions of people. He has frequently appeared on talk shows, has done countless concerts, is successful with both single hits and albums, and is still going strong. What is his story and why has he made it big?

Chapter 1

THE EARLY YEARS

hristopher Jacob Daughtry, born to Peter and Sandra Daughtry, just missed being a Christmas baby, as he was born December 26, 1979. He was born in Roanoke Rapids but grew up in Lasker, both small towns in North Carolina. He lived in Charlottesville, Virginia, and considers McLeansville, North Carolina, his hometown.

Although he now sports a shaved head, Daughtry had full, dark hair when he was just a little boy. In high school, he had a keen interest in both art and drama, and starred in plays and musicals. He had a lot of friends and was pretty popular. He was always able to get along with people. He started working a part-time job when he was thirteen years old, and he worked alongside his father at a sawmill when he was only fourteen. Later, he worked at McDonald's. He was a fan of wrestling, which he and his father used to watch together. Before the *American Idol* audition, he worked at a day job as a service adviser for a car dealership in North Carolina and was part of a rock band.

In his early teens, Daughtry listened to and was influenced by many bands of the nineties. He especially liked grunge bands. Grunge is a style of rock music popularized in the early 1990s that incorporates elements of punk rock and heavy metal. It is often marked by lyrics that talk about dissatisfaction with society. Some of the bands he listened to were Bush, Live, Alice in Chains, and Soundgarden. He liked the honesty of the music, and as a teenager he was probably attracted to some of its messages.

Daughtry also listened to a lot of bands from the eighties, such as Guns N' Roses, Skid Row, and Ace of Base. He also liked hip-hop groups like Public Enemy, N.W.A., Beastie Boys, and House of Pain. He once said that he strayed away from his tastes for a while and became a big Elton John fan, but he always returned to his roots: grunge music.

A Budding Rock Star

Did Daughtry always want to be a rock star? In a *Rolling Stone* magazine interview, he reported that he was looking at a number of career options when he was in high school. He had a talent for drawing and thought he might want to be a comic artist. However, he also liked the idea of being out in front of an audience. Daughtry was into martial arts and toyed with

Axl Rose, frontman for Guns N' Roses, a favorite band of
Daughtry's, performs at the 2002 MTV Video Music Awards at
Radio City Music Hall in New York City.

the idea of being a martial-arts actor like Jean-Claude Van
Damme. But what was always closest to his heart, after he
picked up a guitar at around age sixteen, was the idea of
being onstage.

   According to www.chrisdaughtryweb.com, Daughtry was
told by his best friend, Robert, that he could really sing. They
had to write a song for class, so he was forced to sing in front
of Robert. Daughtry always enjoyed singing but never had
the confidence that Robert gave him that day. They wrote a

On Chris Daughtry Web (www.chrisdaughtryweb.com), you can find the star's latest news, photos, and tour dates.

couple of songs, and he was hooked. He knew what he wanted to do with his life. Robert taught him some guitar chords, and Daughtry took off from there.

Soon after he picked up the guitar, Daughtry started taking singing seriously and started performing with rock bands at Fluvanna County High School in Palmyra, Virginia, where he graduated in 1998. He has also been writing songs since he was sixteen. He has never had any formal singing lessons.

Beginning His Life

After his high school graduation, he continued to play in rock bands. He married Deanna Robertson in 2000 when he was twenty years old. Some people have asked Daughtry if he was ever sorry that he married at a relatively young age. He answers that he felt like he didn't need to look anymore, that Deanna was the woman he felt he was truly supposed to be with. He tells people that if you know that, then just go with it.

Chris Daughtry poses with his wife, Deanna, at the Palms Casino Resort in Las Vegas at a 2007 MTV Video Music Awards (VMA) party.

Daughtry is completely dedicated to his wife. She already had two children, Hannah and Griffin, whom Daughtry took on as his own. His wife was a licensed massage therapist in Burlington, North Carolina. He reports that both their children are musical as well. His daughter loves Kelly Clarkson and Carrie Underwood, two previous winners of *American Idol*. Daughtry also says that his wife is his hero as well as his lucky charm!

He says on his Web site, www.chrisdaughtryweb.com, that Deanna was scared that he was sacrificing his dream by doing that and now she is really excited that he is still getting to live it. Even though he took on the life of a married man and father at an early age, he is still able to live his dream.

The Road to *American Idol*

In 2005, Daughtry felt he was finally ready to take his passion for singing and entertainment to the next level. He performed on the CBS singing competition show called *Rock Star: INXS*. Unfortunately, he did not make the cut for the actual filming of the show. At that time, he was also active as the lead singer for the band Absent Element.

Absent Element was described as having a mind-blowing sound and was compared to bands such as Tool, Sevendust, and Live. Absent Element had started to become a powerful force in creating a unique brand of truly alternative rock. The four distinctively creative and musically diverse individuals that made up the band were Ryan Andrews on bass, Scott Crawford on drums, Mark Perry on lead guitar and backup vocals, and Chris Daughtry on lead vocals and rhythm guitar. Absent Element released the CD *Uprooted* in 2005, which contained the songs "Conviction" and "Breakdown."

After *Rock Star: INXS*, Daughtry still wanted to take his talent to the next level. He was motivated by his wife and decided to audition for *American Idol*. When asked what made him do *American Idol* in the first place, he responded that he was used to playing in small clubs here and there but just did not have

Chris Daughtry tried out for *Rock Star: INXS* before he auditioned for *American Idol*. He didn't make it, but the experience paved the way for his later success.

the audience. There were the set people that came to see his band, but it never expanded. Two of the band members had families to support, as well as jobs; therefore, they could not just get up and go traveling and searching for gigs.

Daughtry decided to take a chance. He went to try out for *American Idol* in Denver and sang the song "The Letter" by the Boxtops. Judges Paula Abdul and Randy Jackson were enthusiastic about his audition, but Simon Cowell was not as thrilled. With two out of three votes, he was passed on to the next level. Part of *American Idol* features highlights from the auditions. Daughtry was featured as he reminded the viewers of Bo Bice and Constantine Maroulis from the previous season. Bice ended up as runner-up, and Maroulis made it to New York City's Broadway starring in *The Wedding Singer*. In fact, Daughtry said he was inspired by Bice to audition for *American Idol* in the first place.

Like Kellie Pickler and Paris Bennett, rocker Chris Daughtry was closely chronicled from the audition round and was a standout favorite from the very start of the finals. Daughtry was highlighted as he was charismatic and handsome. He was also a family man devoted to both wife and children. His audition made a great impression on the judges and on the rest of America.

Chapter 2

ON AMERICAN IDOL

Chris Daughtry was finally in the *American Idol* competition, and he was about to perform on stage in front of millions of people on television. It was February 22, 2006, and Daughtry was really hot when he sang Bon Jovi's "Wanted Dead or Alive." The judges were impressed with his performance. Randy Jackson felt that Daughtry really had it. Paula Abdul gave him a standing ovation, and Simon Cowell felt that it was a positive performance and that Daughtry had a great singing voice but needed to work on his charisma.

After the performance, Daughtry really started building a large fan base. He was not voted off and sang again the following week on March 1. With ten male contestants to go, he wowed the audience with an electrifying performance of his version of the song "Hemorrhage" by the band Fuel.

Wowing the Judges

The judges were unanimous in their praise. Jackson started the comments of the evening by saying that Daughtry's song could be on the radio topping the charts. Abdul was gushing and asking Daughtry if he really knew how good he was. Cowell was impressed, saying Daughtry showed that he was the

The *American Idol* judges *(from left to right)*: Randy Jackson, Paula Abdul, and Simon Cowell. Their often controversial criticisms are part of the reason why the show is such a great success.

standard everyone else should aspire to. With comments like these, everyone, including his fans, felt he was safe and would not be voted off.

Sure enough, Daughtry was back on the show on March 8. He came out strong, passionately singing his version of "Broken" by Seether and Amy Lee. Jackson and Abdul were impressed, but as usual, Cowell was hard to please. He saw Daughtry's performance as boring. This was not how Jackson and Abdul felt, however. Jackson said that he was a fan of Daughtry's and loved the way he stayed true to who he was. Abdul went on to say that no matter what happened in the competition, she was sure Daughtry would soon be selling out shows all over the country. Abdul knew what she was talking about. The audience obviously was not listening to Cowell at this time and voted for Daughtry, who continued on to the March 14 show.

The choice that night was a song by the famous R & B artist Stevie Wonder. Daughtry sang Wonder's "Higher Ground." He incorporated his own style into the song and did wonders as a performer as well. All three judges were feeling Daughtry had made his mark with his genuine performance. Cowell even said that it was the only performance of the night that would stand up in the real world.

Daughtry was safe again, and his performances were getting better and better. The evening of March 21 ended up being a little controversial. The genre was fifties music. Barry Manilow was the mentor to the contestants. Daughtry chose

Award-winning musician Stevie Wonder gave advice to the *Idol* contestants when they performed his songs for the competition. Daughtry sang Wonder's "Higher Ground."

the song "I Walk the Line" by Johnny Cash and sang it in alternative rock style.

The judges were very impressed with Daughtry's rendition of the classic song. Many fans felt that this rendition was very similar to the one done by the band Live, but no reference to Live was mentioned in the broadcast. That got cleared up in the following week. Both Jackson and Abdul praised Daughtry, and Cowell went on to say that Daughtry was the first artist they had on *American Idol* who had refused to compromise. Daughtry knew his strengths and seemed to find a way to turn the genre to his own advantage.

Taking a Risk

On March 28, Daughtry took a risky move. He was truly in his element as he performed heavy metal with Creed's song "What If." He received a lot of criticism for his performance, though. Jackson liked the song but didn't think it was Daughtry's best performance. Abdul, as usual, flattered Daughtry, commenting that she was his biggest fan. Cowell thought that Daughtry went too far as this song was not typically the type that appealed to the American public. He went on to say to Daughtry that he could not keep doing this type of music every night, as this was *American Idol* and Creed's music wasn't the type of music typically heard on the show. Cowell, it appears, right from the beginning, was not a Chris Daughtry fan.

April 4 was country performance night. For a number of contestants, country music was not necessarily their strength. Daughtry sang "Making Memories of Us" by Keith Urban. Again, both Jackson and Abdul appreciated Daughtry's rendition and performance, but Cowell thought the choice was boring.

Daughtry, however, continued to remain popular, and on April 11, he was able to shine with a song by British rock band Queen. Daughtry chose an obscure Queen song called

Simon Cowell is known for being controversial. His comments can provoke strong reactions from the audience. He was critical of Daughtry from the start.

"Innuendo." Cowell was not pleased with the choice and wanted Daughtry to pick one of Queen's more popular songs that the public could identify with. Cowell, though, did force himself to admit that "Innuendo" was done well. Again, Jackson and Abdul became Daughtry's cheering gallery.

April 18 was a bit of a turning point for Daughtry. He sang the song "What a Wonderful World" by Louis Armstrong. Rod Stewart was the mentor for the set. Daughtry demonstrated through his song choice and performance that he could do other styles than solely hard rock. All the judges were in agreement. Daughtry had done a fabulous job. Even Cowell called it great.

Fighting to the Top

After the voting, Daughtry discovered that he was in the bottom three. He was not voted off, but he knew he had to

Chris Daughtry's Song List

Wednesday, February 22	"Wanted Dead or Alive"
Wednesday, March 1	"Hemorrhage (In My Hands)"
Wednesday, March 8	"Broken"
Tuesday, March 14	"Higher Ground"
Tuesday, March 21	"I Walk the Line"
Tuesday, March 28	"What If"
Tuesday, April 4	"Making Memories of Us"
Tuesday, April 11	"Innuendo"
Tuesday, April 18	"What a Wonderful World"
Tuesday, April 25	"Have You Ever Really Loved a Woman?"
Tuesday, May 2	"Renegade" "I Dare You"
Tuesday, May 9	"Suspicious Minds" "A Little Less Conversation"

work harder to get the public votes. On April 25, it was obvious that all his hard work had really paid off. He wowed everyone with his rendition of "Have You Ever Really Loved a Woman?" by Bryan Adams. Before his performance, the audience got a glimpse of Daughtry's new training method. One of his preparations was to lie down on his back to help with opening his chest and singing better. The technique certainly worked. The judges liked this performance and, ultimately, so did the public.

May 2 was a very successful night for Daughtry, and Cowell commented that his performance of the song "Renegade" by Styx was one million times better than his other performances. In Daughtry's second song, "I Dare You" by Shinedown, the strain became evident in his voice; he just was not as strong as he was during his first song. The judges thought that his performance was just OK.

May 9 was a crucial night. It was down to the final four: Chris Daughtry, Katherine McPhee, Taylor Hicks, and Elliott Yamin. It was make-it-or-break-it time. It was Elvis Presley night, and Daughtry rocked out Presley's song "Suspicious Minds." Abdul said that you forget how good "Suspicious Minds" is until you hear Chris Daughtry sing it. She then said to Daughtry that she would see him in the finals. Cowell said simply that the song worked.

Now, like on the May 2 show, Daughtry's first song out-rocked the second song. Daughtry's second song was "A Little Less Conversation." Cowell was not as impressed with this rendition.

Then, on May 10, it came down to who would be the final three contestants. Taylor and Elliott sailed through with no problem. Katherine McPhee and Chris Daughtry were in the bottom two. One of them was going home. Host Ryan Seacrest asked the panel of judges who they thought would be the one going home. Cowell expressed his belief that it would be McPhee. Seacrest read out the name. It was Daughtry who was going home. Many were stunned, including Daughtry. Every one of Daughtry's fans believed the same thing—that he had been robbed of the title but would be around another day. Daughtry may have been kicked off *American Idol*, but it was not over yet! A new chapter was just beginning.

Chapter 3

AFTER THE SHOW

When asked if he was shocked that he was eliminated, Chris Daughtry said that he didn't see it coming, not even a little bit. When host Ryan Seacrest asked him on the show if he was stunned, Daughtry responded that he was. Daughtry's facial expression, however, showed that he was not only shocked and stunned but also terribly upset. He was surprised and felt that he was just being real by expressing on television his true emotions to millions of people. He wasn't going to pretend to be happy about it. He felt that it was definitely a gut-wrenching moment.

He said that it didn't feel good. When asked if he was angry at how Seacrest delivered the news, Daughtry responded that he thought Seacrest was building up the suspense by making the audience think he was going home only to say, "But you can sit down." But Daughtry

American Idol host Ryan Seacrest delivers the news to Chris Daughtry and the audience: Daughtry was going home.

tried to look at the positive. He was trying to be optimistic and see the bigger picture, that there were going to be bigger opportunities in the future.

When asked if he thought *Idol* fans were not ready for a rocker to win, Daughtry commented that it was weird because he had all these people telling him for weeks that it was his for the winning. And when he had so many people telling him that, he assumed that this is what America wanted. The only thing he could think of was that everybody thought he was a shoo-in. Paula Abdul had said that everyone would see him in the finals, so he believed her as well.

Looking Back

Daughtry was asked to reflect about when he had been in the bottom two. In both cases, it was the time he slowed his singing down to more mellow songs. He responded to the question by saying that it made him think the audience wasn't happy when he changed his style. But he felt he was a singer, and a singer can't sing the same song over and over. He felt that there was always a time and place to change things up. He thought as long as he was being true to himself, he was not changing anything other than toning it down a little bit.

Some of the biggest rock bands have done softer songs, so he did not regret slowing it down. When he was interviewed on *The Ellen DeGeneres Show* in November 2006, he told DeGeneres that he had not been expecting to be voted off and said that he had felt like he had been stabbed in the stomach.

Daughtry was asked if he talked to Katherine McPhee after he was told that he was eliminated from the show, as she was the other person at risk of going home. He said at the time he did not, as everybody was speechless and he really did not know what to say. He felt that McPhee had an inclination that she was going to be voted off. Daughtry was in shock, and many millions of Americans were also stunned. The judges also appeared to be in shock. Randy Jackson was very reassuring and said to Daughtry that he was going to be just fine. Abdul was a true believer in him and did not say anything as she was very emotional, put her head down, and appeared to be crying. Simon Cowell did not see it coming and wished Daughtry good luck.

The Fans' Uproar

Many of Daughtry's fans thought that he clearly should have won and were in an uproar. There was some controversy about the vote count as the lines had been down for more than forty-five minutes and the incorrect telephone numbers had been flashed on the screen. There was even an online petition to get Daughtry back. Everyone denied the accusations. When Daughtry was asked why he felt he was voted off, he said that perhaps his fans were overconfident that he would be safe, so they did not call in and vote.

RECOUNT VOTES FOR CHRIS DAUGHTRY Petition

http://www.petitiononline.com/ChrisD06/

Q▾ Google

RECOUNT VOTES FOR CHRIS DAUGHTRY

View Current Signatures · Sign the Petition

FANS DEMAND A REVOTE NOT A RECOUNT!!!

To: American Idol and FOX

Hello Chris Daughtry Fans! This petition is from the hearts of us. We feel that Chris was wrongly kicked off of American Idol on May 10th, 2006. We, the fans of Chris Daughtry, demand American Idol and Fox to do a Recount on the Votes. Ask anyone who they thought was going to win American Idol this year, and 90\% of them would say CHRIS DAUGHTRY. We are shocked and saddened that this has happened. This is a HUGE mistake. Recount the votes American Idol, Recount the votes Fox. You will be greatly surprised that Chris Daughtry should have remained in the competition. If a Recount is not done, with the signatures from all of the Chris Daughtry Fans demanding one, it will only PROVE, that this show is rigged. Please, give us a recount and bring Chris back. HE IS OUR AMERICAN IDOL!!!!!! If you agree with this petition, PLEASE, the Fans urge you to sign it and pass it along to anyone you know who LOVES Chris as much as we do. WE LOVE YOU CHRIS, OUR AMERICAN IDOL!! AND WE WILL FIGHT FOR YOU TO BE THE OFFICIAL AMERICAN IDOL!!!

Sincerely,

The Undersigned

(Click Here to Sign Petition)

View Current Signatures

After Chris Daughtry was voted off the show, an online petition showed up at www.petitiononline.com. Fans were demanding a recount of the votes to get Daughtry back on *American Idol*.

Watching the season you could see that Ace Young and Daughtry were really close. When asked if he had talked to Young after he was eliminated, Daughtry said that he absolutely did. He said that he and Young became like brothers on the show, that they shared similar backgrounds and were strong family men, and that to this day, they continue to have a close relationship. Young called to ask how he was doing, as Young was eliminated previously and had been through the emotional turmoil. Daughtry felt that having a roommate like Young through-out the show and developing a close friendship was a bonus.

Daughtry commented that his wife and kids took the news extremely well. He said that he could not ask for a better family. They always made him feel like everything was OK and did not stress or put pressure on him.

New Opportunities

In May, members of the band Fuel asked Daughtry to join them as their lead singer. He was honored but did not accept. He felt there was going to be a flood of opportunities awaiting him. He reported that there were already some offers lined up but he was feeling all of them out and making sure he was doing the right thing for himself.

He was taking everything into consideration. He did not want to make a rash decision that he would later come to regret. He was a songwriter, so to launch his own career would be his dream, selling out stadiums, and doing his own thing. Daughtry talked about his songwriting. He told people that his writing comes straight from his heart. He said that he writes about his relationship with God; his wife, who inspires most of his lyrics; and other life experiences. He said that if it didn't happen to him, he could not effectively and honestly write about it. Daughtry wanted to combine his talent for songwriting and his dream of forming a band. Looking back, he felt that in the long run it was better that he did not win because he did not see himself

Recording industry legend Clive Davis heads the American division of the BMG music conglomerate. He has guided the debut albums of each of the *Idol* winners.

as a solo entertainer. He always longed to front his own band.

Daughtry's Big Break

Although Daughtry had many offers after May, he did not sign an agreement with RCA Records chief Clive Davis and Simon Fuller's label, 19 Recordings, until July 10. His band would be formed under the name Daughtry.

The band featured guitarist Jeremy Brady, guitarist Josh Steely, bassist Josh Paul, drummer Joey Barnes, and of course, lead singer and guitarist Chris Daughtry. Brian Craddock replaced Brady on the album's release. The top tracks of the album were:

"It's Not Over"
"Used To"
"Crashed"
"Feels Like Tonight"
"What I Want"

Right after he was eliminated, Daughtry appeared on a number of popular shows. When he was on *The Ellen DeGeneres Show*, DeGeneres playfully ripped off Daughtry's shirt to see the brand-new tattoo that he had gotten right after *American Idol*. It said "Daughtry" across his back and shoulders. Ellen said she was disappointed that he was eliminated and predicted that he would eventually become a big star.

On June 8, Daughtry performed a parody of Daniel Powter's "Bad Day" with comedian Jimmy Fallon at the 2006 MTV Movie Awards. On June 16, he made a cameo appearance on *The Tonight Show with Jay Leno* in the Father's Day Gift Ideas segment where he played a father taking out the trash to a talking garbage can.

After *American Idol*, Daughtry's wife, Deanna, commented that music was all her husband ever wanted to do. She said that the public forgets so fast about these Idols once they're off the show. She just hoped they would not forget about Chris Daughtry.

CHRIS DAUGHTRY NOW

Chris Daughtry's debut album, *Daughtry*, was one of the biggest-selling records in America in 2007. In just the first week of sales, Daughtry's album sold 304,000 copies, placing him second behind hip-hop artist Jay-Z, who was number one with *Kingdom Come*, selling 680,000 copies.

Like many hotly anticipated albums of the SoundScan era, Daughtry's album debuted high on the charts, but it did not drop down quickly. It stayed in the top ten month after month after month, as did its first single "It's Not Over." Daughtry said his song "It's Not Over" was one of his favorites. He did it with Greg Wattenberg (who produced Five for Fighting and does A & R for Wind-Up Records).

Success!

The album *Daughtry* was not only a huge hit by *American Idol* standards but also

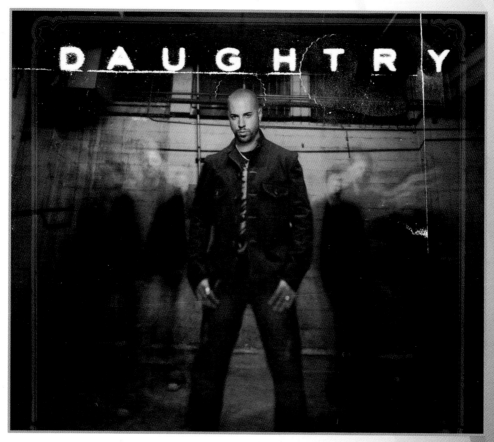

Pictured here is the cover of Chris Daughtry's successful debut album. On it are a number of songs that were written or cowritten by Daughtry.

one of the few hit rock albums in 2006. *Daughtry* was the fastest-selling rock debut in the sixteen-year history of the Billboard album chart's sales tracking system. The album has also been certified triple platinum and is the fifth best-selling digital release of all time.

Chris Daughtry sings the national anthem at the NFL's 2007 NFC Conference Championship game in Chicago on January 21, 2007.

Daughtry admitted that he had been struggling to come to terms with his success since the album hit the one million sales mark. He said, "Sometimes, it never really sinks in where you're at in your career. It seemed so unreal when I found out that we were platinum . . . I was just at home, doing normal everyday stuff at home—taking out the trash, dishes, and whatnot—and I found out we're selling over a million albums . . . It just felt so unreal. It's kind of hard to grasp sometimes."

In the Spotlight

Daughtry continues to appear on television programs such as *The Today Show, Live with Regis and Kelly,* and *The Ellen DeGeneres Show.* On January 21, 2007, Daughtry performed "The Star-Spangled Banner" at the National Football League's NFC Conference Championship game in Chicago. Beginning March 14, 2007, his song "Home" was played every time a participant was eliminated from *American Idol* Season Six. Additionally, on the final competition on May 22, 2007, Daughtry and his new band, Daughtry, performed this song at the end of the show.

On March 23, he performed a free concert in downtown Greensboro, North Carolina. Over six thousand people showed up. On May 25, 2007, Daughtry again appeared on *The Ellen DeGeneres Show*. She gave everyone in her audience a copy of his CD. He told her that he has been touring nonstop since the end of January and just recently had met the *American Idol* Season Six stars. LaKisha Jones, who had recently been eliminated, touched Daughtry's hand for luck, hoping that she, too, would become just as successful as he did.

Daughtry is in demand wherever he goes. Many people think one of the reasons people are so attracted to him is because he has become part of their family. Daughtry commented on this admiration and said that the public really feels like they know you. He was invited into people's homes each week through their televisions. He was also the underdog that appeared to get a bad rap. He may have lost on *American Idol*, but he made it big in people's hearts.

Daughtry felt that it was a little weird how fast everything was happening. It was a year since he went on the show, and before that he had been playing in places for little money and small crowds. When interviewed, Daughtry was asked what was the biggest difference between being a struggling musician and where he is now. He answered that to have people come to see his group and to actually make a living out of it and pay the bills is the best thing. When asked what he thought was the most surprising thing about this part of his career, in the months since the release of his album, he responded that he had been surprised that he could sing every day and that his voice could survive it.

Daughtry says that now that he is on the road doing nightly concerts, he brings with him a picture of his wife, Deanna; his computer; razors for his head; a Bible; and concert clothes. He also does push-ups before each show as he feels that when you get the blood flowing through your body, you have more energy to sing better.

A Newfound Career

Daughtry continues to be busy touring with his band. His concerts have been very successful. For example, tickets to Daughtry's concert at the House of Bricks in downtown Des Moines, Iowa, sold out in two minutes. Daughtry also does club tours. When asked why he books club tours when he can fill much larger venues, Daughtry responded that he didn't want to forget where he came from. This is where he started, playing small clubs. He wanted to do this first to work on the band's stage show as he felt that it was more up close and personal with the fans.

Daughtry continues to play to sell-out crowds wherever he goes. You get the feeling he's still "an event unfolding," wrote one critic about his ability to extend his reach with every performance, a sensibility he's magically been able to capture on the new record. He has been busy testing material in new acoustic songs.

Daughtry continues to stay in touch with some of the other stars from *American Idol*. He talks to Taylor Hicks, Katherine McPhee, Ace Young, Bucky Covington, and Elliott Yamin. People from his hometown describe Daughtry as an unassuming guy who is truly down to earth. The coordinator of Daughtry's support events said that at a time when we have so many bad role models, Daughtry is actually a really good role model for kids and for America.

Daughtry is currently the best-selling *American Idol* contestant who was neither the winner nor the runner-up of his or her season. When asked what his definition of an American Idol was, he answered it was one who worked hard and was a good entertainer.

He has truly worked hard and has shown he is a sensational entertainer. Daughtry commented about his fame by saying that it comes so fast that it is hard to get your head around it. Everyone has a dream. Daughtry's dream was playing music. *American Idol* gave him the exposure, but it is his talent that is continuing the momentum. Does he have it all? With a loving wife and family, a successful career, and a huge heart, what do you think?

The next season is just around the corner. Could you be the next American Idol? Could you be showcased and also follow

Chris Daughtry excites his fans by performing on stage at radio station Z100's Zootopia at Nassau Coliseum on May 18, 2007, in Uniondale, New York.

your dream? As Simon Cowell pointed out, "To be a recording artist selling records around the world is probably the best job anyone could ever hope to have. The business is unpredictable and ruthless, but the rewards are potentially huge. And what makes it all so wonderful is it could be you." Is there another Chris Daughtry out there? Are you the one the public has been waiting for to promote to stardom? Maybe you can have it all as well.

Glossary

alternative rock Also called alternative music or simply alternative, it is a genre of rock music that emerged in the 1980s and became widely popular in the 1990s.

charismatic Possessing an extraordinary ability to attract.

compromise A settlement of differences by mutual concessions.

dissatisfaction A particular cause of feeling of displeasure or disappointment.

gig A job, especially a booking for musicians.

mentor A wise and trusted counselor or teacher.

ovation An enthusiastic public reception of a person, marked especially by loud and prolonged applause.

rocker A performer or fan of rock music.

unanimous Sharing the same opinions or views; being in complete harmony or accord.

For More Information

American Federation of Television & Radio Artists (AFTRA)
260 Madison Avenue
New York, NY 10016
(212) 532-0800
Web site: http://www.aftra.org
> The American Federation of Television & Radio Artists (AFTRA) is a national labor union representing more than seventy thousand performers, journalists, and other artists working in the entertainment and news media.

American Guild of Musical Artists (AGMA)
1727 Broadway
New York, NY 10019
(212) 265-3687
Web site: http://www.musicalartists.org
> The American Guild of Musical Artists, AFL-CIO (AGMA) is an American labor union that represents eight thousand opera singers, ballet and other dancers, opera directors, backstage production personnel at opera and dance companies, and figure skaters.

American Society of Composers, Authors, and Publishers (ASCAP)
One Lincoln Plaza
New York, NY 10023
(212) 621-6000
E-mail: info@ascap.com
Web site: http://www.ascap.com

ASCAP is a membership association of more than three hundred thousand U.S. composers, songwriters, lyricists, and music publishers of every kind of music. Through agreements with affiliated international societies, ASCAP also represents hundreds of thousands of music creators worldwide. Its Web site is a great resource for background info on music.

National Association of Teachers of Singing (NATS)
6406 Merrill Road, Suite B
Jacksonville, FL 32277
(904) 744-9022
E-mail: info@nats.org
Web site: http://www.nats.org

The National Association of Teachers of Singing (NATS) was founded in 1944 and is now the largest association of teachers of singing in the world. Students of NATS members have access to one of the organization's most widely recognized activities: student auditions. They also have the opportunity, along with members, to compete at a national level through the National Association of Teachers of Singing Artist Awards (NATSAA).

Ronald McDonald House
26 Gerrard Street E
Toronto, ON M5B 1G3
Canada
(416) 977-0458
E-mail: info@rmtoronto.org
Web site: http://www.rmhtoronto.org

Ronald McDonald House Charities of Canada (RMHC) is dedicated to helping children with serious illnesses or disabilities and their families lead happier and healthier lives. CTV and the cast of *Canadian Idol* are teaming up to raise funds for Ronald McDonald House.

Save the Children
New York Office
5 Tudor City Place
New York, NY 10017
(212) 370-2461
Web site: http://www.savethechildren.org
American Idol's bold prime-time fund-raising experiment last April resulted in Save the Children receiving $13.5 million to assist children in need in six African countries and in poor communities across the United States.

Web Sites

Due to the changing nature of Internet links, Rosen Publishing has developed an online list of Web sites related to the subject of this book. This site is updated regularly. Please use this link to access the list:

http://www.rosenlinks.com/wyi/chda

For Further Reading

Austen, Jake. *TV A-Go-Go: Rock on TV from American Bandstand to American Idol.* Chicago, IL: Chicago Review Press, 2005.

Cowell, Tony. *I Hate to Be Rude, But . . . : Simon Cowell's Book of Nasty Comments.* London, England: John Blake Publishers, 2006.

Jackson, Randy. *What's Up Dawg? How to Become a Superstar in the Music Business.* New York, NY: Hyperion Books, 2004.

Rich, Jason. *American Idol Season 3: All Access.* New York, NY: Random House, 2004.

Rich, Jason. *American Idol Season 4: Official Behind-the-Scenes Fan Book.* New York, NY: Random House, 2005.

Thompson, Larry A. *Shine: A Powerful 4-Step Plan for Becoming a Star in Anything You Do.* New York, NY: McGraw-Hill, 2004.

Walsh, Marissa. *American Idol: The Search for a Superstar.* New York, NY: Bantam Books, 2002.

Bibliography

American Idol. "Chris Daughtry." Retrieved September 1, 2007 (http://www.americanidol.com/contestants/season5/chris_daughtry).

American Idol Worship. "Chris Daughtry." Retrieved September 1, 2007 (http://www.americanidolworship.com/categories/chris-daughtry).

AOL Music. "Daughtry Biography." Retrieved September 1, 2007 (http://music.aol.com/artist/daughtry/815153/biography).

Chris Daughtry Fans—An Official Fan Site. Retrieved September 1, 2007 (http://www.chrisdaughtryfans.com).

Chris Daughtry Web. Retrieved September 1, 2007 (http://www.chrisdaughtryweb.com/about.html).

Cowell, Tony. *I Hate to Be Rude, But . . . . : Simon Cowell's Book of Nasty Comments.* London, England: John Blake Publishers, 2006.

Gundersen, Edna. "It's Just Beginning for Chris Daughtry." *USA Today.* Retrieved September 1, 2007 (http://www.usatoday.com/life/music/news/2007-03-20-chris-daughtry-main_N.htm).

Mervis, Scott. "Booted from Last Year's *Idol* Chris Daughtry Has Last Laugh with Chart-Topping Album." *Pittsburgh Post-Gazette.* March 25, 2007. Retrieved September 1, 2007 (http://www.southcoasttoday.com/apps/pbcs.dll/article?AID=/20070325/LIFE/703250366).

Index

About the Author

Sandra Giddens is a true *American Idol* fan. She especially enjoyed Chris Daughtry on the show. She is a special education consultant at the Toronto District School Board. She has her doctorate in education and has written a number of books for Rosen Publishing. She is looking forward to the next season of *American Idol,* but in the meantime, she is watching *Canadian Idol* and *So You Think You Can Dance.*

Photo Credits

Cover, pp. 1, 5, 25 © Vince Bucci/Getty Images; p. 9 © Frank Micelotta/Getty Images; p. 11 © John Shearer/Wirelmage/Getty Images; p. 13 © Frederick M. Brown/Getty Images; pp. 16, 20 © Kevin Winter/Getty Images; p. 18 © Ann Johansson/Getty Images; p. 30 © Bryan Bedder/Getty Images; p. 34 © Al Messerschmidt/Wirelmage/Getty Images; p. 38 © Mat Szwajkos/Getty Images.

Designer: Tahara Anderson; **Editor:** Nicholas Croce
Photo Research: Amy Feinberg